THE COLOUR OF BLACK & WHITE

For Reference

Do not take from this room

Liz Lochhead was born in Motherwell, Lanarkshire, and educated at Dalziel High School, then Glasgow School of Art 1965–1970, when she graduated with a D.A. from the Department of Drawing and Painting. Her first collection of poems was published in 1972 and since 1978, when she gave up teaching art in secondary schools (at which she was terrible) she has been a full-time writer.

A playwright since the early 1980s, she has written for all of the major Scottish and some English theatre companies a score of plays, both original dramas and translations or adaptations. Original plays include *Blood and Ice*, *Quelques Fleurs* and the award-winning plays *Mary Queen of Scots Got Her Head Chopped Off* and *Perfect Days*. Translations and adaptations include versions of Moliere's two greatest comedies in rhyme, Chekhov's *Three Sisters*, the *York Mystery Plays*, and *Thebans*, an adaptation of both Sophocles' *Oedipus* and *Antigone* linked by *Jokasta*, from material mainly out of Euripides' *Phoenician Women* – this seamless trilogy for Theatre Babel to premier at the Edinburgh Festival Fringe 2003. Her published version of Euripides' *Medea*, which was comissioned and performed by the same company, won the Saltire Book of the Year Award in 2001.

She is in demand all over Britain and internationally as a performer of her own work and she is a frequent broadcaster, especially on Radio Four.

This, Liz's fifth collection of poems and her fourth book with Polygon, fulfils a life-long ambition to work closely with a great Scottish printmaker on an illuminated book.

Memo for Spring (Reprographia, Gordon Wright 1972)

The Grimm Sisters (Next Editions 1981)

Dreaming Frankenstein and Collected Poems (Polygon 1984)

True Confessions (Polygon 1985)

Bagpipe Muzak (Penguin 1991)

Penguin Modern Poets Four (1995 with Roger McGough and Sharon Olds)

A Choosing (Polygon 2011)

Published Plays

Blood and Ice (Methuen Plays by Women Four 1984)

Mary Queen of Scots Got Her Head Chopped Off (Penguin 1988)

Dracula (Penguin 1988)

Quelques Fleurs is published in *Scotland Plays* (Nick Hern Books 1998)

Perfect Days (Nick Hern Books 1998)

Cuba along with *Dog House* by Gina Moxley (Faber & Faber 1999)

Medea: an adaptation from Euripides (Nick Hern Books 2000)

Miseryguts and *Tartuffe*: rhyming translations of Moliere's *Le Misanthrope* and *Le Tartuffe* (Nick Hern Books 2002)

Thebans from Sophocles' Oedipus and *Antigone*, Euripides' *Phoenician Women* (Nick Hern Books 2003)

THE COLOUR OF BLACK & WHITE

Liz Lochhead

Lino & Woodcuts
by
Willie Rodger

POLYGON

First published in Great Britain in 2003 by Polygon,
an imprint of Birlinn Ltd.

Reprinted 2005, 2009, 2011, 2012, 2014

West Newington House
10 Newington Road
Edinburgh
EH9 1QS

www.polygonbooks.co.uk

ISBN 978 0 954407 52 0

British Library Cataloguing-in-Publication Data
A catalogue record for this book is available on request from the
British Library.

Design by James Hutcheson

Typesetting and origination by Brinnoven, Livingston
Printed and bound by Bell & Bain Ltd, Glasgow

POEMS

LINO AND WOODCUTS

Acknowledgements

Some of these poems, in slightly different forms, have previously appeared in *Bagpipe Muzak* (published by Penguin Books, now out of print) or in *Poetry Review* or *Chapman Magazine* or have been broadcast on Radio Four. The author is grateful for the Cholmondley Award for Poetry she received in 2002. And very grateful, too, to have been awarded a Residential Fellowship by the Civitella Ranieri Foundation in 2000 when she worked on some of these poems while a guest in their artists' studio accommodation in Umbria.

To Tom Logan, and to Tom Leonard

I

The Unknown Citizen

How to exist
except
in a land of unreadable signs and ambiguous symbols
except
between the hache and the ampersand
except
between the ankh and the ziggurat
between the fylfot and the fleur de lys
between the cross and the crescent
between the twinned sigrunes and the swastika
or the sauvastika its mirror image, its opposite –
meaning darkness/light whichever –
with a blank page for a passport

except
under some flag
some bloody flag with a
crucially five
(or a six or a seven)
pointed star?

The Man in the Comic Strip

For the man in the comic strip
things are not funny. No wonder he's
running in whichever direction his pisspoor
piston legs are facing
getting nowhere fast.

If only he had the sense he was born with
he'd know there is a world of difference
between the thinks bubble and the speech balloon
and when to keep it zipped, so, with a visible fastener.
But his mouth is always getting him into trouble.
Fistfights blossom round him,
there are flowers explode when the punches connect.
A good idea is a lightbulb, but too seldom.
When he curses, spirals
and asterisks and exclamation marks
whizz around his head like his always palpable distress.
Fear comes off him like petals from a daisy.
Anger brings lightning down on his head and
has him hopping.
Hunger fills the space around him
with floating ideograms of roasted chickens
and iced buns like maidens' breasts the way
the scent of money fills his eyes with dollar signs.

For him the heart is always a beating heart,
True Love –
always comically unrequited.
The unmistakeable silhouette of his one-and-only
will always be kissing another
behind the shades at her window

and, down-at-the-mouth, he'll
always have to watch it from the graphic
lamplit street.

He never knows what is around the corner
although we can see it coming.
When he is shocked his hair stands perfectly on end.

But his scream is a total zero and he knows it.
Knows to beware of the zigzags of danger,
knows how very different from
the beeline of zees that is a hostile horizontal buzzing
of singleminded insects swarming after him
are the gorgeous big haphazard zeds of sleep.

In the Black and White Era
for Ian McMillan

'Hitchcock,
there was a Hitchcock on.' he said. *'Lifeboat.*
I'd harped on about it that much that Dad and I
had stayed up late to watch it.
Cocoa, and there we were, father and son in
nineteen-fifties checky dressing gowns and striped pyjamas.
Mum was up late too, footering with the packing
because next day we were going on our holidays.
The big black and white TV
was a boiling box of cruel grey sea,'
he said, 'when the door went.
We were normally such a family of early bedders too,
and my Mum was all for not answering –
the time of night and us going our holidays tomorrow –
which wasn't a bit like her, not normally,
and obviously – door went again, and then again –
wasn't going to be on, now was it? So
when she changed her tune from
"Don't go, Jack," to "You better go, Jack,"
Dad tied his cord again tighter and went to answer it.

What I remember, and I do remember
whatever my Mum says, and though my Dad denies it,
is the man sitting there on our settee,
sitting there the way no visitor ever sat,
not normally, without so much as a cup of tea
and a biscuit, which was unheard of, with that big dog of his
wetly wolfing down the water my mother –

and this wasn't like her – had so very grudgingly
brought it in that flowered bowl I'd never seen before.

"I've never seen you before in my life,"
said my Dad to the man. And, honestly
it wasn't like him to be blunt like that.
This was after the man looked long at him and said,
"I know you, you're Jack Jones, I was
on the same ship as you, Ark Royal, remember?"
My Mum was wringing her hands and saying,
"A fine time of night this is to come to folk's door –
and here they're away on their holidays tomorrow too!
You with your shaggydog stories of walking to Hamilton
and needing a bowl of water for your dog.
The doorstep wasn't good enough for you, was it?"

The TV was still on. *Lifeboat*. Which, with
a visitor in, it wouldn't have been, not normally.
A Hitchcock I never saw the end of,
not that night,
and as far as I know has never been repeated.'

Ira and George
for Michael Marra

'First the phonecall'
as the man said – and he sure said a mouthful –
to that 'which comes first, words or music?' question.
Who knows? Except: for every good one
there are ten in the trash, songs you slaved over
that just won't sing, in which no lover ever
will hear some wisecrack twist itself to tell
his unique heartbreak (so sore, so personal)
        so well
he can't stop humming it. The simplest three chord
        melody might have legs
once it's got the lyric, not tunesmith's
        ham-and-eggs.
Each catchphrase, colloquialism, each cliché
each snatch of overheard-on-the-subway or
        street can say
so much, so much when rhymed right, when
        phrased just-so to fit
its own tune that was born for it.

A Manhattan night in twenty-nine or thirty.
It's late, you're reading Herrick. Just back
        from a party,
your brother calls out 'Hey let's work!' You
        watch him shuck
his jacket, loose his black-tie and grab your book.
'Gather ye rosebuds' he says, and slams it
        shut. He's right.
Hard against the deadline and at night –

shoes off, moon up (just daring you),
                              piano open –
that's when you two can make it happen.
The tune that smells like an onion? Play
                              it very
slow, then *the one that sounds like the
                              Staten Island Ferry*
till you hear the words – brother, they're
                              already there
under the siren and the train and the cab
                              horn blare
of his jazz of endless possibilities that will
                              only fit
its own fine-tuned lyric that is born for it.

The Beekeeper
for Carol Ann Duffy

Happy as haystacks are my quiet hives
from this distance and
through the bevel of this window's glass.
This is the place I robe myself
in net and hat and gloves.
This is my vestibule,
crocked like a dairy, full
of the sexual smell of bees.

Bees that fizzle out singly
like smoke rising from one cigarette
then straighten-up and fly right
hauled
by olfactory magnets
while, loaded, laden,
their fellow workers make a beeline home.

This is the business
and I mind the time the old man,
showing me my first stuffed queen, the
tawny intricate purpose moving on the quiet comb,
made me initiate of this gold, this goodness.
He taught me the riddle of Samson –
Out of the strong came forth sweetness –
the honeycomb in the lion's carcase.

Out of the eater comes something to eat
Out of the strong comes something sweet.

I flip my net back
and go bare-armed on and out to them
wishing only to trust my own good husbandry
and do nothing
nothing but feel them
crawl and trawl the follicles, stamens
and pistils of my unpollened arms.

The New-married Miner

My shift is over that was night time all day long.
My love, it's lowsan time. Alone among
these dog-tired colliers my drouth's for home.
Bank up the fire with small coal till I come
and before tomorrow I'll not think again
how sore and small the space I have to hunker in
or how huge and hard but true it pulls all day
as at the pithead, black against the sky,
the big wheel turns. Now my bike's
coggling front wheel clicks and squeaks,
my cold bones ache as hard for home I pedal
still blacked up like a darky minstrel.

My long path home is starved of light
so I must do without.
No moon tonight, so round and white –
its Davy Lamp's gone out.
Frost edges every blackened leaf,
black snot-flowers on my handkerchief.

Heat my bath scalding
and, bonny lass, I'll make
the white lace of the lather black.
Squeeze the hot soapy flannel
at the nape of my neck
and scribble long white chalkmarks down my back.
Put the dark fire to the poker
till the hot flames burst in flower.

Stretch out the towel and I'll stand up.
Hold and fold me
rub and scrub me as hard as you can
till in your white warm arms I'll end up
a pink and naked man, my love
                    your pink and naked man.

The Baker

I am as lucky for a funeral
As a sweep is at a wedding
When with his red eyes, furred brush and burnt smell
He blesses bridal lace with his soil and smirching.

Thus do my work-night whites,
The cracks on my dusted boots,
My overall trousers of flour-stiffened linen
Handsel your black ties and pressed mourning suits

Although I am not by your side, nor
Does any one photograph my – or that rawest – absence.
Dawn delivery to this hotel had me
Shoulder those boards of my generous dozens

As all week neighbours came with bakestuffs
Up the saddest path to your door
Wanting to bring something sweet and light
To where nothing can be so any more.

And now I sleep on sacks washed soft
While you – your time at the cold grave over,
Or after that stare at the core of the terrible oven –
Take tea and funeral cakes together.

Let sober girls in black and white replenish plates
And freshen up the cooling cups with warm
As if tomorrow like live yeast could rise and prove.
I say: such crumbs do no harm.

In nights while I will work and you will grieve
Weak tea, sudden hunger for the heel of a new loaf,
White dawn and the surprise of appetite
Will have you tear a lump of goodness off.

Sooner, later a new season's wind will lift –
Though it may be many daily loaves from this dark hour –
As you let go, fling, and feel the ashes sift
Around your footsteps like spilt flour.

II

Kidspoem/Bairnsang

it wis January
and a gey dreich day
the first day Ah went to the school
so ma Mum happed me up in ma
good navy-blue napp coat wi the rid tartan hood
birled a scarf aroon ma neck
pu'ed oan ma pixie an' ma pawkies
it wis that bitter
said *noo ye'll no starve*
gie'd me a wee kiss and a kid-oan skelp oan the bum
and sent me aff across the playground
tae the place Ah'd learn to say
it was January
and a really dismal day
the first day I went to school
so my mother wrapped me up in my
best navy-blue top coat with the red tartan hood,
twirled a scarf around my neck,
pulled on my bobble-hat and mittens
it was so bitterly cold
said *now you won't freeze to death*
gave me a little kiss and a pretend slap on the bottom
and sent me off across the playground
to the place I'd learn to forget to say
it wis January
and a gey dreich day
the first day Ah went to the school
so ma Mum happed me up in ma
good navy-blue napp coat wi the rid tartan hood,

birled a scarf aroon ma neck,
pu'ed oan ma pixie an' ma pawkies
it wis that bitter.

Oh saying it was one thing
but when it came to writing it
in black and white
the way it had to be said
was as if you were posh, grown-up, male, English and dead.

Little Women
for Carol Ann Duffy and Jackie Kay

When Oona Cody left me
for that new girl Helen Derry
initially
I had everybody's fullest sympathy –
which entirely failed to comfort me.
That Helen Derry, yon one,
her with the wee fur cuffs on her bootees, the
knife edges on her accordion pleats which,
when she birled to swing them
in a quick scart along the peever beds
or bent to touch her toes, showed
a quick flash of her scut
in pants embroidered with the days of the week.
Rumour was she'd plain refused once to come to school
with Thursday on on a Monday and ever since –
oh, she was a hard case that Helen Derry –
her mother had learned her lesson, taken
a tumble to herself, got a grip and shaped up
good and proper.

My mother was predictable.
If that was the kind of friend Oona was, well,
she was no friend of mine, good riddance,
she was somebody anybody,
anybody with a bit of sense,
would be glad to see the back of.
Which was, wasn't it, just what a mother *would* say?
And everybody in the class said the novelty would wear off.
'Bide your time' and 'She'll come running back'

these seemed to be the bromides of conventional wisdom.
And Helen Derry, as for her, she could
get back to where they called Levoy 'Bendulum'
(Bendulum!)
and Dutch ropes 'French' and she could just
take her wee blue bottle of Evening-in-bloody-Paris
back with her, coming here breaking up the
true marriage of a best friendship
with her face like the back of a bus
and her bahookey like the side of a house
and the wings on the famous specs you couldn't get on the
                                                    N.H.S.
and the 'auntie an airhostess'
and the wee lucky birthstone pierced earrings, the monster.

But I knew everybody knew what I knew.
There was something wrong with what I'd had with Oona.
Although the sanctity of our togetherness had seemed
                                                    unbroken
and her content – I'd thought – to swap scraps
with no thought of anyone else or anything 'missing' –
us able to run the gauntlet of a three-legged race in perfect
                                                    step together
with hardly a knot in the hanky that yoked us together.
Now I was bad luck, bad luck altogether.
No wonder all the other couples avoided me,
frantically spooling themselves into each other tightly
with loving lassoos of the french-knitting that ravelled
                                                    endlessly
from the wee dolly-things that were all the craze
and they worried at like rosaries.
'There but for the grace of God' and
'Please, please let it never happen to me, so help me' –

seemed to be the size of it as they jumped double bumps
together,
arms down each other's coatsleeves, and chewed each other's
used bubble gum for luck and love.
What the magazines said was that this was a chance,
a chance to be truly honest with yourself
and see where you had gone wrong, or slipped up,
or let yourself go, or taken things for granted,
been lax about 'communicating' – for how many
of us could say we really took the time to talk or listen?
The magazines reminded that revenge
was a dish better eaten cold (and then you'd see it was only
good taste to leave it).

For Oona Cody's birthday – the first anniversary
since she'd left me – I bought her a copy of
Louisa May Alcott's two best-loved children's classics,
Yes, 'Little Women',
'Little Women' and 'Good Wives' in a Compendium
Edition
with a green marbled cover and one frontispiece,
a great book
I knew Oona – my Oona – would definitely love.
She was sitting under the pegs at playtime,
under the pegs with Helen Derry,
the both of them engrossed – or acting-it engrossed,
for God-knows-whose benefit though, so
(with hindsight) I'll concede it likely they *were* in
a mutual bona-fide brown study – engrossed
in a wee free-pamphlet entitled 'Growing Up'.
I clocked the cover (two doves and a butterfly
above the – open – gates of womanhood
with the pastel-coloured coloured-in country beyond).

And Oona Cody had the grace to blush
when I dropped the present – all wrapped up –
like a reproach in her lap.
I held my breath till lunchtime, when –
Helen Derry stood against the railings, watching –
Oona Cody marched up to me and said she didn't want a
        birthday present,
not from me, and anyway Helen had already read it.
'She says it's pure morbid, the wee sister dies
and the boy-next-door marries the wrong one,
the eejit that talks French and sleeps with
a clothespeg on her neb to improve her profile into aquiline
and thinks of nobody but herself and flaming art.'

So I had to go home with it,
home to face my mother's scorn,
to stick it up on the shelf beside the identical one I had already
knowing I'd never have the neck to take it back and swap it
for 'What Katy Did' & 'What Katy Did Next'
but was stuck with it –
' *"Christmas won't be Christmas without any presents," grumbled Jo,
lying on the rug.'*

The Metal Raw

was what we used to call
what must've really been the *un*metalled road or row,
a no-cars scratch across two farmers' tracts
between ours, with its brand new scheme,
and the next
ex-mining village.

At four, or five or six or so, I thought
it meant the colour, though. *Metal raw*
was crude red (*rid*) gravel that you'd
better not brake your bike on and that surfaced
just the first hundred yards or so
then patched the worst of the ruts
on the dirt and mud and clinker of the rest of it. Rust
on corrugated iron, that was *metal* and *raw*, both.
A real remnant of *The Iron Curtain* for all I knew,
torn and gouged with nail holes along edges
that you'd to *watch they wouldnae rip the hand off you.*

Sheets of this stuff crumbled to red dust along the Metal Raw
among the black cold fires and rags and bits of brick
around the place the tinkers still camped
a week or two each Spring
with their piebald ponies.
Always some story
among us weans around the scheme or at the swings
about somebody's big cousin creeping close enough
to kick the boiling billycan over, about a shaken fist,
cursing and swearing and how far, on the light nights,
that big man with the stick had hunted him.

I was wee enough then,
on a Sunday walk along the Metal Raw
with Mum and Dad in my good coat,
for the tinks' big black dog that *wouldnae do me any harm*
to knock me flying in the mulchy ditch among
flag iris and the reeds I called *bullrushes*
and that might have harboured Baby Moses
and not one bit surprised me.
See, I am talking of the time when I mixed up
Old Meg she was a gipsy
and that old woman up the Metal Raw
smoking a pipe outside a tilting lean-to of tarred and
patched tarpaulin stretched on hawthorn.

And this was the nineteen fifties.
We slept under a *mushroom cloud*,
feared *Kruschev and Bulgarin*, men in Cossack hats
in blizzards of interference on the tiny grey T.V. screens
of *the Cold War.*

This was the time when our mothers down the New Houses
stood on *Red Cardinal* doorsteps
far too scared not to buy the tinkers' pegs and prophesies.

Lanarkshire Girls

Coming into Glasgow
in our red bus through those green fields. And
Summer annoyed us thrusting
leafy branches through the upstairs windows.
Like a boy with a stick through railings,
rattling us. We bent whole treetops
squeezing through and they rained down twigs, broken
bits of foliage, old blossom on the roof,
chucked hard wee balls of unripe fruit,
drumming us out of the country.

Then it was
shabby schemes, gospel halls, chapels, Orange halls,
doctors' surgeries, the crematorium, the zoo,
gap sites where August already frittered the stuffing out of
unpurpling fireweed and splintering thistles
till the blank blue sky was dot-dot-dotted
with whiskery asterisks.

Soon the coherent cliffs of Tollcross,
the many mansions of those lovely red and
blackened tenements. Our country bus sped
past the city stops, the women in their
slippers at the doors of dairies,
the proud pubs on every corner, accelerated
along the glamorous Gallowgate, juddered by
Reeta's gallus fashions and the
gorgeous dragons of Terry Tattoo Artist, till it
spilled us out, fourteen years old, dreaming ourselves up,
with holiday money burning a hole in our pockets
at the corner of Jamaica Street.

Your Aunties
for Elizabeth Miller

your Auntie was
famous for being an air hostess or
famous for being a nurse
famous for being a bloody good sport
famous for being a Pain in the Erse
famous for being able to take a joke or
famous for Quite the Reverse.

famous for the office sweepstake and spectacular wins
your Auntie was
famous for her perra stoatin pins
famous for her big blue eyes
famous for her brass neck
famous for her mince pies
her harangues, her meringues, her am-I-right-or-am-I-wrangs?
famous for her talent contest
famous for Always Doing her Best
famous for For-Christssake-Wullie-will-you-give-it-a-rest?

famous for her bra
famous for her good bones
famous for her tattie scones
famous for her foxtrot
famous for her scarlet lipstick
famous for her scarlet fever
famous for Always Getting Up at Weddings and
              Singing The Twelfth of Never.

famous for *turning*
famous for being a poppet
famous for being a Nippy Sweetie
famous for Always Being Im*ma*culate
or
famous for being a bloody mess
famous for the specs you couldn't get on the N.H.S.
famous for Signing the Pledge at the Bandy Hope
famous for her famous *esperegus* soup.

famous for being as daft as a brush
famous for fast thinking
famous for . . . What-do-you-think?
famous for her driving
famous for her drinking
famous for famously driving your Uncle Freddie to drink.

famous for the Famous Grouse
famous for her bought house
famous for her High Ideals
famous for her peerie heels
famous for her natural curls
famous for her Toni
famous for her fake tan
famous for her Wee Man
famous for her canary
famous for being the salt of the Earth
famous for being phoney
famous for being *gen*uine
famous for being a poser
famous for being a Literary Creation like Aunt
       Julia The Auntie of Mario Vargas Llosa
famous for her Giaconda Smile

famous for making scenes
like a Dickensian Aunt
or a Wodehouse Aunt, a Dylan Thomas
or a Graham Greene's . . .
famous for being Norman MacCaig's Gaelic Aunt
        Julia in her black box bed
or Edwin Morgan's Aunt Myra at a tea dance in the
        twenties with a new tune in her head
famous for being one of Alan Bennett's
                Bradford Aunties who were
famous for I-take-as-I-find and
always-speaking-me-mind and
not-being-taken-in-by-t'-toffs
famous for being Charlie's Aunt
or Roger McGough's . . .

A very well known phrase or saying
meaning you are
welcome to whatever you want is:
Eat up – you're at your Auntie's!

Clothes
for Helen Simpson

There are dresses – good dresses,
dresses you always loved –
that are suddenly so clean gone
they never become a duster or
leave so much as a square of themselves
rubbing around decades later in the ragbag.
This was what I learned listening
to my mother and my aunts
when on one of the good days in the long Summer holidays
they sat out on backdoor steps
or – skirts spread out – on a tartan rug
on the back green under the white sheets
hung high. 'What *happened*
to that wee dress?' one of my aunts
would ask my mother or she'd ask them
coming out of one of the fridgeless kitchenettes
of the fifties with a jug of Boston cream
saying 'Johnnie aye liked me in that costume . . .'

Maybe it was my grandmother saying
'That was a good coat that'
with all the reverence and gravity
remembrance of such a garment
was rightly due. You knew how true it was
she liked *good things*. When someone said
'That was something I always felt right in . . .'
what you heard was the real regret, the yearning.

If something could be explained away
as having been worn till it was well and truly *done*

this would dismiss it from discussion.
But the mystery of that *wonderful swagger-coat* –
a *great* coat – left on a train in the nineteen thirties
that *disappeared before it was gone back for*
only minutes later
was enough to make it mythical to me
as Joseph's Coat of Many Colours,
as the one dream dress every one of them had danced in
and no one was sure who it actually belonged to or
whatever happened . . .
You learned that everything was in the detail,
that their mouths made rosebuds
to recall *rows of toty-wee covered buttons.*
Their knowledgeable eyes narrowed at *darts*
or *edge-to-edge, bugle-beading, Peter Pan collar,*
gleamed when they as much as said *sateen.*
Something had never been 'blue' but
saxe or *duck-egg* or 'a shade somewhere
between *peacock* and a *light royal*
almost an *electric blue* – but no as gaudy' . . .
Talk was of *barathea, grosgrain, watered taffeta*
organza, covered coating.
When it came to this stuff *stuff*
every one of them was her mother's daughter.
I'd say every sister had three sisters
who were women after their own hearts

if I didn't remember my youngest aunt, the looker –
the one who later divorced and remarried,
with the perfect eyebrows
and who never had a bad perm or a tint that
went metallic, harsh, who never had fireside tartan
or visible veins measling her legs in their glassy nylons –

smoothing down the glazed cotton over net
splashed with huge impossible blue roses,
admiring the *this-year* almond toes
of her gorgeous gunmetal shoes
and saying nothing

while her mother and her sisters argued enjoyably
over a past no one could quite agree the colour of
and that might or might not have been
                    sprigged with tiny flowers.

Social History

My mother never
had sex with anyone else
except my father. A week before
her three day leave to get married
my mother was examined by the Army Doctor
and pronounced *virgo intacta*
twenty four years old and virgo intacta
an unusual thing in the ATS
an unusual thing in wartime
if you believe even half of what you read
in the social history books.
And the joke was I wasn't even sure
your Dad was going to make it. Rumour was
they were going to cancel all leave prior to D Day
so it was touch and go till the last minute . . .

The sex my mother could've had
but didn't
sounded fantastic. Clever Jewish boys
from the East End of London
whirled her round the dance floors
niftily slow foxtrotting her into corners
telling her the khaki matched her eyes.
A soldier in a darkened carriage on a slow train
wept on her shoulder when he told her
that he'd lost his brother in North Africa.
Two naval ratings on Margate pier
slipped a string of cultured pearls in her pocket
said 'Miss, we just found these on the beach
and you are so pretty we thought you ought to have them.'
She had a very close and very tender

friendship with a lovely, lovely gentle N.C.O.
from the North of England who told her she was
the image of his girlfriend. An Italian
prisoner of war sketched her portrait and
her sister who had her eye on him
was quite put out.
She didn't care for Yanks but that didn't
stop them trying. A Free Frenchman
fell in love with her. A Polish Airforceman
proposed. Any Scotsmen she met
down there had lovely educated accents
and tended to be Top Brass.
She mixed with folk from All Over.
Which was the beauty of the services
and the best of the party that was wartime,
while the buzzbombs overhead didn't quite
cut out.
She was quite capable of downing her half of bitter
and rolling out the barrel with all the other girls
without ending up squiffy up against the wall
afterwards with her knickers down, unlike some.
When they all rolled back to barracks late,
swinging their lisle-stockinged legs
from the tailgate of a lorry singing Appleblossom Time,
Military Policemen turned a blind eye
in exchange for nothing more than a smile.
Officers messed around with her in the blackout,
but then my mother told them
she was engaged to be married to my father
and they acted like the officers and gentle-
men they were and backed off sharpish, so

my mother never
had sex with anyone else
except my father, which was a source
of pride to her, being of her generation
as it would have been a source
of shame to me, being of mine.

After the War
for Susanne Ehrhardt

After the war
was the dull country I was born in.
The night of Stafford Cripps's budget
My dad inhaled the blue haze of one last Capstan
then packed it in.
'You were just months old . . .'
The Berlin airlift.
ATS and REME badges
rattled in our button box.

Were they surprised that everything was different now?
Did it cheese them off that it was just the same
stuck in one room upstairs at my grandma's
jammed against the bars of my cot
with one mended featherstitch jumper drying
among the nappies on the winterdykes,
the puffed and married maroon counterpane
reflected in the swinging mirror of the wardrobe.
Radio plays. Them loving one another
biting pillows
in the dark while I was sleeping.
All the unmarried uncles were restless,
champing at the bit
for New Zealand, The Black Country, Corby.
My aunties saved up for the New Look.

By International Refugee Year
we had a square green lawn and twelve-inch telly.

Sorting Through

The moment she died, my mother's dance dresses
turned from the colours they really were
to the colours I imagine them to be.
I can feel the weight of bumptoed silver shoes
swinging from their anklestraps as she swaggers
up the path towards *her* dad, light-headed
from airman's kisses. Here, at what I'll have to learn
to call *my father's house*, yes every
ragbag scrap of duster prints her even more vivid
than an Ilford snapshot on some seafront
in a white cardigan and that exact frock.
Old lipsticks. Liquid stockings.
Labels like *Harella, Gor-ray, Berkertex*.
As I manhandle whole outfits into binbags for Oxfam
every mote in my eye is a utility mark
and this is useful:
the sadness of dispossessed dresses,
the decency of good coats roundshouldered
in the darkness of wardrobes,
the gravitas of lapels,
the invisible danders of skin fizzing off from them
like all that life that will not neatly end.

1953

All the Dads, like you, that spring
had put the effort in.
Stepped on it with brand new spades
to slice and turn
clay-heavy wet yellow earth
to clods that stank of clay
and were well marbled
with worms and rubble.
You set paths straight
with slabs it took two men to lift.
Tipped barrowloads of topsoil. Riddled.
Sowed grass seed from illustrated packets
that showed tall flowers, long English lawns
striped green like marrows. Then
stretched over paper bowties on strings
to frighten birds.
So gardens happened
where the earth had been one raw wound.

And behind whitened windows
the Mums were stippling walls
or treadling Singers as they
ran rivers of curtain material
through the eye of a needle and out again,
fit to hang by Coronation Day.
This was in rooms
that had emptinesses, possibilities,
still smelled of shaved wood
and drying plaster.

In no time at all
in a neat estate a long time later
I will watch in a dawn
through a crack in drawn curtains
this lawn, the late September borders,
mature roses
and the undertaker coming up the path
carrying a pint of milk.

III

View of Scotland/Love Poem

Down on her hands and knees
at ten at night on Hogmanay,
my mother still giving it elbowgrease
jiffywaxing the vinolay. (This is too
ordinary to be nostalgia.) On the kitchen table
a newly opened tin of sockeye salmon.
Though we do not expect anyone,
the slab of black bun,
petticoat-tails fanned out
on bone china.
'Last year it was very quiet . . .'

Mum's got her rollers in with waveset
and her well-pressed good dress
slack across the candlewick upstairs.
Nearly half-ten already and her not shifted!
If we're to even hope to prosper
this midnight must find us
how we would like to be.
A new view of Scotland
with a dangling calendar
is propped under last year's,
ready to take its place.

Darling, it's thirty years since
anybody was able to trick me,
December thirtyfirst, into
'looking into a mirror to see a lassie
wi' as minny heids as days in the year' –
and two already since,
familiar strangers at a party,

45

we did not know that we were
the happiness we wished each other
when the Bells went, did we?

All over the city
off-licences pull down their shutters,
people make for where they want to be
to bring the new year in.
In highrises and tenements
sunburst clocks tick
on dusted mantelshelves.
Everyone puts on their best spread of plenty
(for to even hope to prosper
this midnight must find us
how we would like to be).
So there's a bottle of sickly liqueur
among the booze in the alcove,
golden crusts on steak pies
like quilts on a double bed.
And this is where we live.
There is no time like the
present for a kiss.

Neckties

Paisleys squirm with spermatozoa.
All yang, no yin. Liberties are peacocks.
Old school types still hide behind their prison bars.
Red braces, jacquards, watermarked brocades
are the most fun a chap can have
in a sober suit.

You know about knots,
could tie, I bet, a bowtie properly
in the dark with your eyes shut, but
we've a diagram hung up
beside the mirror in our bedroom.
Left over right, et cetera . . .
The half or double Windsor,
even that extra fancy one it takes
an extra long tie to pull off successfully.
You know the times a simple schoolboy four-in-hand
will be what's wanted.

I didn't used to be married.
Once neckties were coiled occasional serpents
on the dressing-table by my bed
beside the car-keys and the teetering
temporary leaning towers of change.
They were dangerous nooses on the backs of chairs
or funny fishes in the debris on the floor.
I should have known better.

Picture me away from you
cruising the high streets
under the watchful eyes of shopboys

fingering their limp silks
wondering what would please you.
Watch out, someday I'll bring you back a naked lady,
a painted kipper, maybe a bootlace
dangling from a silver dollar
and matching collarpoints.
You could get away with anything
you're that goodlooking.
Did you like that screenprinted slimjim from Covent Garden?

Once I got a beauty in a Cancer Shop
and a sort of forties effort in Oxfam for a song.
Not bad for one dull town.
The dead man's gravy stain wasn't the size of sixpence
and you can hide it behind your crocodile tie pin.

A Night In

Darling, tonight I want to celebrate
not your birthday, no, nor mine.
It's not the anniversary of when we met,
first went to bed or got married, and the wine
is supermarket plonk. I'm just about to grate
rat-trap cheddar on the veggie bake that'll do us fine.

But it's far from the feast that – knowing you'll be soon,
and suddenly so glad to just be me and here,
now, in our bright kitchen – I wish I'd stopped and gone
and shopped for, planned and savoured earlier.
Come home! It's been a long day. Now the perfect moon
through our high windows rises round and clear.

IV

Epithalamium
for Joe and Annie Thomson

For Marriage, love and love alone's the argument.
Sweet ceremony, then hand-in-hand we go
Taking to our changed, still dangerous days, our complement.
We think we know ourselves, but all we know
Is: love surprises us. It's like when sunlight flings
A sudden shaft that lights up glamourous the rain
Across a Glasgow street – or when Botanic Spring's
First crisp, dry breath turns February air champagne.

Delight's infectious – your quotidian friends
Put on, with gladrag finery today, your joy,
Renew in themselves the right true ends
They won't let old griefs, old lives destroy.
When at our lover's feet our opened selves we've laid
We find ourselves, and all the world, remade.

The Bride

I am the absolute spit of Elsa Lanchester.
A ringer for her, honestly,
down to the zigzag of lightning in my frightwig
and it's funny no one, me in-
cluded, ever noticed the resemblance before
because
this fine morning
jolted awake by a crash in the kitchen
the smell of burning
and the corncrake domesticity of dawnchorus toast
getting scraped, suddenly
there's the me in the mirror staring back at me
and me less than amazed at me all marcelled
like Elsa Lanchester.
Well, it's apt enough,
this is my last morning as a
single girl.

Despite your ex-wife's incendiary good wishes,
there's the new frock I've been dieting into for
more than a fortnight
quite intact
over the back of the chair.
And because last night was my last night,
last night I left you,
left you to your own devices under the double duvet
and went home to home-home
to sleep my last night in my own
single bed.
I'd love to say I've my own
old toys around me, et cetera and the same old old-

gold counterpane, but is it likely?
Is it likely what with the old dear's passion
for continuous redecoration?
There's not so much as a Sundayschool prize
not long gone to Oxfam –
just one wall-eyed
teddybear some rugby player gave me for my
twentyfirst
and an acrylic still life with aubergine
(which for one moment I consider asking for –
except where could we hang it?)
to take home to our home, our
old home which today's nuptials must make
our new home,
take home to remind myself of what I can't remember
which is what the hell the girl who did that picture
and was as far as I can remember
painting-daft
has to do with me,
the me with the Lanchester look.

Breakfast.
Breakfast on a tray and like a
condemned man I
can have anyting I want for
breakfast, but
before I can lop the top off my boiled egg,
before I can say soldiers far less
dunk them, the place is
bristling with sisters
stripping me and unzipping me
and down the hall the bathroom taps are pounding
Niagara and bubbles.

'Bucks Fizz three fingers cheers kiddo cheerio'
this is Ellen
the older one
the matron of honour
clashing glasses knocking it back
in her slip and stocking soles
plugging in her Carmens
drenching herself in the Dutyfree Diorissimo
Dave brought back from that refresher course in
Brussels with his secretary
unpacking Mothercare plastic carriers
of maximum security sanitary protection from
her Antler overnight case because
she never knows the minute
with that new coil she had fitting after Timothy.
And Susan
our Susan
sixteen, sly eyes and skinny as a wand she's
always fancied you,
ecru and peach, apple green satin she'll
take all the eyes even though it's meant to be
My Day,
the bizzum's in kinks over the under-
crotch buttons of my camiknickers and I'm
to touch nothing till that
Hazel comes to comb out my hair.
Mother is being very mother-
of-the-bride, rushing round squeezing
Euthymol-pink shrimp-flavoured creamcheese
on platters of crackers bigger than millwheels
and though her daughters all agree
a donkey brown twopiece is somewhat
less than festive

at least we're all thankful she's not
drawing squinty seams up the back of her legs
with eyebrow pencil
in memory of her wedding
in nineteen forty-three.

And here's the taxi
and I stretch up my arms
like one beseeching heaven
like one embracing fate
and four sets of hands help me into my dress
my dress I don't want to wear
my dress that after the whole kerfuffle
is really nothing special
my dress that, should you jilt me
leave me in the lurch at the altar of the registry office
tilting my
fragile psyche
for ever permanently agley,
the dress I'll have to wear for ever
till I'm dafter than Miss Havisham
in mourning for my life until it rots under the oxters.
I should have
chosen really carefully.

And then with Dad in the taxi
and I know
it's going to crash because there's got to be
something
going to stop me from ruining my life like this
but no,
no Dad winks and one swig
from his hipflask and we're bowling

gaily down the aisle towards you,
you and the best man I've been
knocking off for yonks
with his grin
and the ring
and his pockets
bulging obscenely with apocryphal telegrams.

Because we have opted for a
Quiet Wedding
and a civil sort of civil ceremony
the front four pews are chocabloc with
all our old lovers
who (since we've taken
so long to tie the knot) have all been
married to each other, separated, been
divorced so long
they're on really friendly terms again and
surely someone,
someone will declare some
just impediment to stop this whole ridiculous
charade?
I make my vows
but all the time I'm screaming
'No No No' I
hear a voice
a voice I'm sure I recognize to be my own voice
loud as you like 'I do'.

Despite
the unfortunate business at the
Reception and the
manageress's Jack Russell

depositing that dead rat right at my satin slippers
under the top table while
(animal lovers to a man) the company
applauded laughed and cheered –
despite
the fact that when we came to cut the cake
it collapsed
like a prizewinning office block
in a spectacular shambles of silver
cardboard Ionic columns and white
plasterboard icing sugar we got
into the going away car while the going
was good and now,
now here we are
alone at last
in the plumbed-in-twin-
bedded room of this hotel
where we told the man we'd booked a double
but he smiled shrugged said
he'd no record of that and this was all they had
so take it or leave it.
So we did.

We unpack
our paperbacks. We
scorn such sentiments such institutionalizing as
making love on this our wedding night
and it's only
after (sudden lust
having picked us up by the scruff of the neck and
chucked us into
that familiar whirlpool) and
practised and perfect

we judder totally together
into amazed and wide-eyed calm and
I lie beside you
utterly content that I know for sure
that this is never
ever going to
work.

The Redneck

The day I got married I was like a rake.
Six month on the popcorn diet. Starving
but I wouldn't give the girls at work the satisfaction.
All so as I could swan down the aisle in my Scarlet O'Hara
towards that pig with a knife stuck down his sock.
Kilt suited him, but. Unlike ma da.
A toss-up between the Ancient Buchanan
and the Hunting MacIntyre.
I wanted tartan yes but no too roary.
State I was in everything had to be just so.
I had my mammy roasted in a pinwheel hat.
Ended up whole thing was nothing but a blur
and him shouting 'Perfect Working Order'
every two minutes mooning his mates
and flashing the photographer with his
Lion Rampant boxer shorts. A right rid neck.

During my marriage I ballooned.
None of a family thank God.
Bad enough splitting up without the complications.

The Bridegroom

is a necessary
accessory –
if often irrelevant
a bit of a white elephant
after the event.

He should be tall, but not *too* tall – the ideal's
tall enough to top but not
tower over her in her highest high heels.
He should, at the risk of being banal,
have quite a pleasant personal-
ity, be well-built
in morning suit and top hat (or tuxedo . . . or kilt)
whichever
but he'll never, however
nice his smile
or perfect the profile
next to her in the getaway car
be more than a penny stick of licorice
to her sixpence worth of candyfloss
– the bride's the star!

He's of frankly secondary importance to the dress.
Not optional but an extra
nevertheless.

Yup, the role of bridegroom as they scatter
the confetti's
a bit of a bit part – but *husband*, don't forget, is
ha! another matter.

V

Two poems on characters suggested
by Bram Stoker's 'Dracula'

1. Lucy's Diary

I

When the big car came for me
I could have sworn I still smelled
my dad's cigar as I leaned back among the leather.
When Jim and the porter sweated to heave
my locked trunk into the back I shrugged
that this was my last time for leaving.
My scorn was all for those
sentimental girls who pressed
keepsake handkerchiefs and cameos and cachou-
boxes into each other's hands and wept and kissed.
I did not look back as we drove off.

Near Birmingham,
red dust, the smoke from my father's factories.
The sunset extra beautiful because polluted.
Dark and a thin, thin moon
by the time we reached seven, the Crescent,
Whitby. Sitting pretty on its cleft cliff.

II

Heartwood is gloomy.
Mama and I quarrel, constantly.
She says I vex her toying with my fork
but imagine if something on your plate
had been a bird once,
well I can't

eat that!
I'll not pick at so much as one feather of flesh,
never. My mother!

Mourning is only a hair brooch
and a heavy dress she will put on.

III
Yesterday
the gardener's big lad
gave me a peach from the greenhouse.
Unthinking, I bit and sucked
then suddenly flung it from me
in a real rage at its beauty.
Something in its furred blush hurt me,
stuck in my throat
like a lump and made me spill,
deliberately,
clouded paint-water all over my watercolour
I'd worked on all morning, spoiling it.

IV
I walk and walk and walk.
Florrie says that dog
doesn't know it's born now I'm back.
I wish I were as thin and clean
as that tinkerish boy I caught out today
scudding back with a daft grin –
he must've been all of ten –
from whitecap waves to squirm
into his dirty clothes again.

I'd like to swim far out, not drown.

V

I don't like
the way I look.
I will freckle far too easily, my hair
just won't do the right thing.
When Quincey Morris calls me mighty pretty
it only makes me hate him.

I tilt at
the big, big oval mirror in its mahogany.
This gross flesh I will confine
in the whalebone of my very own
hunger. All term
I would not bleed, not
for Matron, Mama, Mademoiselle,
nor my sister Mina.

VI

Despite myself,
the sea air is giving me an appetite.

2. Renfield's Nurse

When I go in to him
I never know what to expect.
I move in antiseptic corridors.
I come bearing a bedpan like a begging bowl.
I bring hot water, carbolic, huckaback.
I bring a hypodermic, a bowl
of brown stew I've saved for him special,
or three dicey horse pills
rattling like chance in a plastic cup.

Times
he'll be nice as ninepence
sitting up smiling
that pink and bland you'd
swear he'd all his marbles.
Lucid as the next man.

Others
when he doesn't know me from Adam –
though he's always got a glad eye for the girls.
I blame the uniform.

Sometimes
he cowers in his own dirt in the corner
whimpering
Doctor don't you hurt me Doctor.
I say it's just the nurse
I say come on you know it's only me.

He looks up at me
with them dog eyes and says
you the nice one or the nasty 'cause I never
know what to expect?

My hands are gentle.
My starched apron cracks
like a whip hand.

VI

5th April 1990
for Edwin Morgan on his 70th birthday

Today I got back from Berlin and the broken Wall.
With bits of it.
Smithereens of history, the brittle confetti
of chiselled-off graffiti,
trickle on to the brave blue dogeared cover
of my signed copy of *Sonnets from Scotland*
that I had with me and have just unpacked.
It hasn't travelled well, but crumbled,
this souvenir I brought for Fünfzig Pfennige
picked out from the brightest chips,
from the priciest slabs with names
or obscenities half intact – all on offer
from that grinning gap-toothed Kreuzberg
Gastarbeiter kid who really thought
he had it made.
Well, he saw me coming all right –
another dumbcluck tourist
taking the slow curve of the Wall
towards Mariannenplatz, gawping at
the Bethanien-House artists mending
still-serviceable slogans on what was left standing.
This was a facelift the
chinking chisels of stonepeckers would
only worry at in turn and yet
they painted, and lovingly,
as if these fluorescents and enamels
would last one thousand years
and make good sense.

Every night I spent at Wannsee
at the Writers' House by the Lake,
Morgan's poems whirled me from space
to the bedrock of my own small
and multitudinous country, swung me
through centuries, ages, shifting geologies
till I was dizzy and dreamed
I was in the sands of the desert and the dead
as the poets lived it, just before my time,
then I was following Gerard Manley Hopkins
in priestly black up North Woodside Road
like a taunting Irish boy till I was suddenly,
stone cold sober, contemplating De Quincey
out of his mind in Rottenrow.

And all there was was
the symmetry of these turning pages,
fourteen lines mirroring fourteen lines,
the small circle of light
from the Bauhaus lamp on my borrowed desk
and the sough of trees in the Grunewald.
And outside there was Berlin.
The moneychangers at Zoostation
fanning out fistfuls of Ostmarks,
little lozenges of polystyrene, drifts and
spills from the packaging of dragged
video recorders and ghettoblasters,
blown white as hailstones and as light as popcorn
about their feet.

There was the wasted acreage of the Polish market
beside the Nationalgalerie where
the Ein' Mark, Ein' Mark, Ein' Mark

everything cost was so slow coming in
some of these sellers-in-hell bought
bottles of berry vodka from fellow blackmarketeers
with all they'd made and more, gave up,
got too blitzed to even pretend
to peddle bits of tractor, tools, laces,
mushrooms from polluted fields
bashed tins filched from hungry Warsaw,
bumpy Eastern European school shoes
to the haggling Turkish families from
the U-bahn's Istanbul Express.

And now I'm home
with three painted Polish Easter eggs,
Hungarian opera duets, Romanian symphonies,
an uncopyrighted East German Mickey Mouse
painted the wrong colours,
funny tasting chocolate
and the Rolling Stones 'in ctepeo'
Made in Bulgaria *Made in the Shade.*
And bits of the wall that are almost powder.
I think who could make sense of it?
Morgan could, yes Eddie could, he would.
And that makes me want to try.

aquarium 1

in the fin-
de-siècle gloom
of the berlin aquarium
what little what thick
light we move through (so
slowly) is
underwater green.

lugubrious big fishes
in cross sections of small ponds
bump blunt noses
against their world's end.
there are razorbills, swords, pigsnouts, fronds,
metallics, micas, twists of tiffany glass –
impossible in this changed air to say
what's animal, or vegetable, or mineral.
louvred shoals flicker open shut off on
are gone.
one's a
tilted tin box
articulated awkwardly,
the next is a sinuous slip-of-a-thing
swivelling through tattered café curtains of bladderwrack
with a torchsinger's pout
to a bugeyed audience of
little fish who roll their eyes as if to say
get this
and gasp with just-too-regular-
to-not-be-phoney
openmouthed surprise.

things pulse
like hearts and lungs
in hard-to-look-at
medical programmes on your home aquarium
and anemones bloom and close
in fast photography through
day night day night day night day
five unshrivelling seasons every minute.
here are the lurid tentacles
of amazing latex nineteen-fifties
Woolworth's swimming caps.
there is a real
ripper's peasouper
encased in a green glass box
and in it
one obscene frill ripples.

and this, this
is neon graffiti
writing itself, wiping itself
on a wall of water.

aquarium 2

everything
looks more alive
than a crocodile
even the
slimy reptilian turds
of the crocodiles
more likely to slither
or the lumps of terrible meat
nacreous with the iridescent
sickness of the pearl on their
cruel red stumps rejoin and walk
than this shrivelled elbow or
these claws engage not a
splash or even a bubble in this
dire stink you cannot breathe in.

but the ragged long mouths
of the crocodiles and their various
species and snouts
are as indistinguishable and divers
as the sleeping hatreds of europe
and you cannot tell what crocodiles
are made of any more than the
sleeping hatreds of europe
(whether bark or hide or barnacled stone
ancient and primeval and awful)
but these sleeping monuments
are alive and dangerous
as the sleeping hatreds of europe.

three visits

one was eighty seven and huggin john and jane
at tegel then in his big beatup munich car to tadeusz'
open house on schlesische strasse slam bang against the
hard fact of the wall and schlesische tor the end of the line
for gastarbeiters tadeusz' place and the coffeepot that
never emptied kreuzberg kids in and out the trickle of the
wheels of rolf's bike as as he brought it in undoing cycle clips
and reaching for a beer and berlin lou reed's berlin belting
out big speakers in berlin by the wall you were five foot
ten inches tall it was very nice candlelight and dubonnet
on ice but it was extra ouzo all round for us at the greek
across the road where any friend of tadeusz was a friend
of the boss and tom and I slept
back in my artschool days it seemed in a borrowed
flat next door where old beaded dresses hung across
the wall in a tangle of bedclothes on the floor newbuild
newbuild newbuild with tom and john and jim arguing
architecture architecture architecture and it was
berlin 750 jahre and the biggest bigdipper in europe
checkpoint charlie where tom was stopped two hours for
carrying in mcniven's tape he wanted us to post in the east
to his musician friend boiled cabbage and you must hang up
coats in the cloakroom in the palace of culture and queue
to go up the fernsehturm to see the whole divided city
spread out below ugly ugly alexanderplatz and die
dreigroschenoper at the berliner ensemble which felt
exactly like the citz death and destruction in detroit
at the schaubühne which didn't and walls came up
enclosed us queenie lying on the floor four hours long the
play and her belly huge two weeks before louisa we stayed
up all night dancing and took the plane home reeling drunk.

two was george wylie a bird is not a stone a christmas
schoolkids' sculpture project at the wall schmuck and trees
glühwein and sugared cookies in the cold cold glittering
square around gedächtniskirche ka de we brandied fruits
like jewels jewels like brandied fruits frozen wannsee
to friedrichstrasse and duty free whisky to take to the
east berlin poetry reading in the pottery where the wheel
turned and the poets were illegal and it was nearly the
darkest day of the year the first snow of winter
nineteen eighty eight.

three was after the wall was opened and one single city
amazed
and bursting at the seams in nineteen ninety

Almost-Christmas at the Writers' House

Morgan, master of the Instamatic Poem,
has flung open the glass door
– three storeys up –
of this high guest suite, and,
his own camera cocked and ready,
flashgun primed,
is muttering 'Mag-ritte, Mag-grrritte'
with a mock-burr and much glee.
About to freeze-frame the scene before him.

Untouched by even a spring of birdclaw,
perfect behind wrought-iron battlements,
twenty or thirty feet of
snowy rooftop
sports a chair and round terrazzo-table
tipsily iced with an inches-deep drift.
Directly opposite
behind another rooftop door
which mirrors this,
lit up by slicing beams of anglepoise
but quite, quite empty this late at night
is the beautiful Bauhaus calm
of the office of the director of the
Literarisches Colloquium.

Behind Morgan,
Withers, Mulrine, McNaughtan, Lochhead,
well-clad, scarved and booted
stamp and laugh
(impatient for Gulaschsuppe and Berliner Weisse
at the restaurant by Wannsee S. Bahnhof)

then breathe, stilled
as his shutter falls, stopped
by this one moment's
crystalline unbroken vision
of the dreaming order in the
purring electric heart of the house of our hosts.

VII

Good Wood

hardwood
softwood.
sapwood
heartwood.
firewood
dyestuffs coal and amber.
bowls broomhandles platters textile rollers
maple sycamore wildcherry gean.
paperpulp brushbacks besomheads horsejumps
birch.
alder clogs a certain special charcoal
used in the manufacture of gunpowder.
spindles dogwood skewers.
cricket bats fine willow charcoal for artists' use.
hornbeam ox-yokes
mallets cogs and butchers' chopping blocks.
walnut gunstocks
tableware veneered interiors.
poplar and aspen woodwool
chipbaskets matchsticks and matchboxes.
chestnut hop poles posts and stakes.
blackthorn walkingsticks
(the traditional shillelagh).
wattle wattlehurdles
peasticks beanrods heathering hazel-withes and hoops.
ash tennis
racquets billiard cues and hockey sticks.
holly for turnery inlaid work and marquetry.

larch planking.
linden hatblocks and pianokeys.
grand fir noble fir douglas fir spruce cypress pine
pitprops paperpulp packing cases
roofing flooring railway sleepers and telegraph poles.
bathtime fragrances of cedarwood and sandalwood.
oak tanning pigmast panelling
and scottish fishing craft.
elmwood coffins in damp earth might warp won't split.

Papermaker
for Jacki Parry at Gallowgate Studios

Rags and flowers perhaps.
What goes into the mulch of memory
is what does not always
grow on trees.

Linen, worn cotton, tattered silk are proper
for the making of fine new paper.
It must have a history
the grind of this hollander
can macerate to what is truly permanent.
Then what pulps, what fluffs of fibres!
Nothing but pure water will gloriously
plump and floss.

What do you love most of all?
Is it the gathering and beating of the fibres?
Or feeling Japanese to be in the morning marshes
gathering cattail-reeds for papermaking,
begging banana-leaf at the botanics,
hanging sheaves of marrams and marshgrasses
from your ceiling like good-cook's herbs
in a giant's kitchen –
singing 'oh I am like the barley
bags of silk'?

The long hairs of inner bark,
the essentials of feather, seed, leaf, grass,
are not like
the industrial slurry of woodpulp and linters
(this too you love:
bleached, maybe,

dyed brilliantly).
Is it best to be more than elbow deep
in the swirled mucilage of the vat
agitating to perfect suspension
every last particle
before you panhandle with your mould and deckle?
Or is it, a minute later,
to know again your own surprising strength
when you, only just, win out against
the dreadful, draining suck
of tonweight water pouring from the mould?
You smile to yourself
satisfied to see a substance
obeying its own laws, cleaving to itself,
every fat fibre loving fibre
when you flip it, single, coherent
brand new on the blanket.
It is like a snowfall,
the first thinnest layer,
almost enough for just one snowball.

What will you make of it?
Rainmaker,
seabeach in a box,
pages from a diary,
wordless books?

Pails of dense dyes, bowls of pulp.
In the big sink continuous water drips.
Stirred up, the vat reeks of flax dams.
Unshelved
the new Japanese books concertina open
still smelling of kozo, mistumata, gampi.

A Wee Multitude of Questions
for George Wylie
On his 75th birthday

Who is the man
'it pleases as much to doubt
as to be certain'?

Whose faith
is in the questioned faith?

Which Great Scot
(pronouncedly Scottish) pronounces
Scul?ture
most Scotchly with a question mark and a
glottal stop?

Who puts a question mark at the centre of everything?

Who lives unbowed under the slant of Scottish weather,
loves the white light of stones,
walks on wiry grass
and, feeling the electric earth beneath him,
turns his wide gaze to the open sea?

Who was the young sailor
who walked in a place of ash and char, fused glass, bone?
Who saw that, aye, rocks *do* melt wi' the sun
and let pulverised granite run through his fingers
like *the Sands of Time shall Run?*
(The name of the place was
Hiroshima
and in the middle of the word
was the hugest question-mark.)

93

Who will surely
interpret for us the monograms of the stars?

Who is the man
whose name belies his nature?
(for 'wily' he is not; there is
craft in it, and art, but no guile. He is true
and straight, his strategy is honesty, and to ask –
in all innocence
in all experience –
the simplest, starkest, startling
questions.)

Who makes biting satire out of mild steel?

Who wishes to avoid Incorrect Assumptions leading to
False Conclusions? Wants us to question mark,
yen, buck, pound?

Who in *A Day Down A Goldmine* asked us to resist
the Golden Fleece, the Big 'I-con'
that would swizz us all to sell our souls?

Whose
Berlin Burd
faced an absurd
obstacle?
(Which the bird keeked over
and The Wall keeled over.)

Who, one Christmas, made
gorgeous guano-free robins
cheep in George Street, Edinburgh,

more multitudinous
than were starlings once in Glasgow's George Square?

Which George is the Captain of *The Question Mark*
and Daphne his first mate?

Whose Jubilee
was happily misspelled *Jubliee* on page thirty-five
of his lovely, jubbly, jubilee catalogue?

Who decided a locomotive might descend a staircase
and a tramcar might have wings?

Who made the out of order
Standing Stones walk?
Who made Holyrood into almost Hollywood
for the Festival Fringe?

Whose spires inspire us,
unquestionably celebrate?

What the devil was the de'il
wha danced away wi the exciseman?
(Art did! Art is the very devil that danced
awa wi the exciseman.)

Who is the Mad Professor up all night in the attic
inventing *The Great British Slap and Tickle Machine*?
Who is our ain
National Genius, wir true Caledonian McBrain?

Who speculates about what is
below the surface, douses, divines?

Whose rod is not a Y
but a why? Whittled to a ?
(His *'by hook, by crook'* he advances with, slowly
over rough ground in his good grasp;
his shepherds crook;
his boat hook
hauling us aboard – hang on to your sou-westers,
shipmates, it'll likely be a bumpy ride.)

In the dark spaces of our heads
divers, multitudinous, unmarked, the questions float
above a straw locomotive and a paper boat.

Warpaint and Womanflesh
for Lys Hansen, painter

because the flesh can be
tortured
because the flesh can be
raped
because the flesh can be
mutilated
because the flesh can be
burned
because the flesh can be
scorned
because the flesh can be
corsetted within the skin
because the rage can be
held in
the flesh must be painted.

because the skin can be
displayed
because the skin can be
flayed
because the skin can be bruised used abused
gorgeously gored gilded
pierced grafted grazed greased
split slit skelped scuffed stretched scratched scored stroked
caked with make-up
tanned tattooed tabooed
because the skin
can be the tip of the iceberg
because
the skin

can be the bag with all the boiling blood and bones within
the skin must be painted.

because the lip can be
any of your and all of your
old lip
because the lip is tender
because the lip can slip
because the lip can kiss and tell
because the lip can frame the mouth that is the mouth of hell
because the lip can be
lipsticked slicked smeared larded lauded glossed bossed
                                                breached
because the lip can be zipped
the lip must be painted.

because of the white of the eye
because of the white lie
because of the truth of the colour of fire
because of the iris of desire
because
the limb can be akimbo
the limb can be dismembered
because the love can be remembered
because the lady can be sawn in half
because the lady can bellylaugh
because the lady's got guts
because the lady's not for turning
because of the good times
because of the war crimes
because of the iron maiden
because of the presidential wink
because of everything except the kitchen sink
Lys Hansen must be always painting.

The Journeyman Paul Cezanne
on Mont Sainte Victoire
for James Runcie

What do I paint when I paint the blue
vase, the hanged man's house,
the still life of Hortense's hands
arranged on the still life of her lap,
domestic arabesques
of the red armchair, petrified drapery,
this mountain?
I paint
the blue in the blue
the red in the blue,
the violet in the gold,
this mountain.
The cylinder, the cone, the sphere,
this mountain.
In the light of perfect logic
this mountain built of paint more permanent than stone:
constructed.

An apple, an orange, a ball, a head –
every day this mountain.
When that critic called me 'a carpenter
with paint', he did not insult
this journeyman!
Colour can move, can make, mountains.

VIII

Year 2K email epistle to Carol Ann Duffy, Sister-poet & Friend of my Youth

Duffy, I'm *fifty-two* – how come?
I'm a wife. You're over forty and a mum.
Clichés like *tempus fugit, yeah it's going some*
Fall from our lips.
– While into each new moment, day, millennium
Your Ella skips.

Ella skips. Time marches on. We're history
By two thousand and something or other, A.D.
If *forward though we canna see*
We guess and fear,
We'll live as though we don't, OK? From me –
Happy New Year.

Black and White Allsorts
for Jackie Kay

a liquorice bootlace
a cultured pearl necklace
a little black dress
lux flakes, snowflakes
sno-pake, tippex
a black bra
a zebra, an op-art umbrella
ebony, ivory, black Sobranie, a skunk
a black eye, a white feather, a pool of printers ink

a brand new *broderie anglais* bikini
pasta al nero di seppia (squid ink linguini)
one single earring of jingling jet
and, like a big black sugar-cube, a perfect *briquette*
black suede boots just out of the box
and, to go with your good black patent shoes, pet,
new white socks

coconut, caviar, a wee pet lamb
a jar of home-made blackcurrant jam
spilt salt, wet tar, black ointment, The Broons
a box of Black Magic and an old black-and-white
on a Sunday afternoon
a white dove
a long black glove
a scoosh of mousse, the full moon
a soot crust, a snowball, a Lee's macaroon
a meringue, mascara, a dollop of Nivea
talc on black lino

the (shuttered) dark
a dropped domino
a white angora bolero
two daft dalmations in the snow
in Kelvingro-
ve park

Hell for Poets

It's Hell for the poet arriving for the gig
Off the five thirty three to meet the organiser
Who claps her in a car that reeks enough of dog to make her
          gag,
Tells her he's *looked at her work* but he was none the wiser.
Call him old fashioned, but in the 'little mag
He edits for his sins' stuff *rhymes* – oh, he's no sympathiser
With this modern stuff! Is it *prose*? What is it?
Perhaps the poet can enlighten him this visit?

– For which his lady-wife's made up a futon hard as boulders
In the boxroom. 'So much *friendlier* than an hotel!'
Will anyone turn up tonight? Shrug of his shoulders.
'Even for *McGough* or *Carol Ann Duffy* tickets have not been
          going well . . .'
Meanwhile: here's *his* stuff, each ode encased in plastic in
          three folders.
Publication? Perhaps she'll advise him where to sell
Over a bottle of home-made later? Oh shit. She can tell
This is going to be The Gig From Hell . . .

But it's real hell for *real* poets when love goes right
When the war is over and the blood, the mud, the Muse
          depart
Requited love, gratified desire 'write white'
And suffering's the sweetest source for the profoundest art.
Blue skies, eternal bliss, bland *putti* – Heaven might
Not be the be all and end all . . .? For a start
Hell itself's pure inspiration to the creatively driven.
Hell was (f'rinstance) Dante's idea of Hog Heaven.

Hell's best! Virgil knew it too before him. Heigh ho!
Man calls himself a poet? St Peter'll bounce him
(Unless he's maybe Milton – it's Who You Know.)
Could I end up in Hell with Burns (his rolling r's announce
                                        him)?
End up with Villon, Verlaine, the Rabelaisian Rimbaud,
With Don Juan, *Don Whan* – however you pronounce Him –
Bunked up with Byron, still so mad, so bad, and so delic-
iously dangerous to know? Not a snowball's chance, but oh,
                                        I wish.

Almost Miss Scotland

The night I
Almost became Miss Scotland,
I caused a big stramash
When I sashayed on in my harristweed heathermix onepiece
And my 'Miss Garthamlock' sash.

I wis six-fit-six, I wis slinky
(Yet nae skinnymalinky) –
My waist was nipped in wi elastic,
My powder and panstick were three inches thick,
Nails? Long, blood-rid and plastic.
So my big smile'd come across, I'd larded oan lipgloss
And my false eyelashes were mink
With a sky blue crescent that was pure iridescent
When I lowered my eyelids to blink.

Well, I wiggled tapselteerie, my heels were that peerie
While a kinna Jimmy Shandish band
Played 'Flower of Scotland' –
But it aw got droont oot wi wolf whistles –
And that's no countin 'For These Are My Mountains'
– See I'd tits like nuclear missiles.

Then this familiar-lukkin felly
I'd seen a loat oan the telly
Interviewed me aboot my hobbies –
I says: Macrame, origami,
Being nice tae my mammy –
(Basically I tellt him a loat o jobbies).
I was givin it that
Aboot my ambition to chat

To handicapped and starvin children from other nations
– How I was certain I'd find
Travel wid broaden my mind
As I fulfilled my Miss Scotland obligations.

Well, I wis in Seventh Heaven
To be in the Final Seven –
But as the Judges retired
To do what was required
And pick the furst, second and thurd
Well, the waiting was murder and it suddenly occurred there
Was something *absurd*
Aboot the hale position
Of being in competition
Wi other burds like masel
Who I should of kennt very well
Were ma sisters (at least under the skin)
Yet fur this dubious prize I'd have scratched oot their eyes
And hoped they'd git plooks, so I'd win!
Aye, there wis somethin ridic'lous
Aboot sookin in wi thae prickless
Wonders o judges, their winks and their nudges.
Wan wee baldy comedian bloke
Whose jokes were a joke:
Wan heuchter-choochter singer who wis a dead ringer
For a cross between a pig in a tartan poke
And a constipated bubblyjock:
Plus wan wellknown soak –
A member of our Sporting Fraternity
Who was guaranteed his place in Eternity
As a well-pickled former member of the Scotland Squad.
And the likes of them were Acting God,
Being Real Men,
Scoring *us* on a scale of one to ten –

They'd compare and contrast, and then at last
They'd deign to pronounce
And reverse-order-announce it.
Then I wid simper, look sweet, an
I'd burst oot greetin
Gasp 'Who me' – the usual story –
They'd plonk me down, stick on the Miss Scotland crown
To crown my crowning glory.

How would *thae guys* like to be a prize –
A cake everybody wanted a slice of –
Have every leering schoolgirl consider them a pearl
Everybody kennt the price of?
How would *they* like their mums to say that their bums
Had always attracted the Ladies' Glances,
And nothing wrang wi it, they'd aye gone alang wi it
And encouraged them to take their chances?
And they were Good Boys, their Mum's Pride & Joys,
Saving it for their Future Wives?
And despite their fame they still steyed at hame
And lived real clean-living lives?

In a blinding flash I saw the hale thing was trash
– I just Saw Rid
And here's whit I did:

– Now I'd love to report that I was the sort
To speak out and convince the other lassies
Pick bones wi aw the chaperones
And singlehandedly convert the masses
Till in a bacchanalian Revenge of the Barbie Dolls

Crying 'All for One and One for All!'
We advanced on the stage, full of bloodlust and rage –
But, I cannot tell a lie, the truth is that I
Just stuck on my headsquerr and snuck away oot o therr –
I know I did right, it wisnae contrary –
And I let my oaxters grow back in
Really rid and thick and hairy.

Because the theory of feminism's aw very well
But yiv got tae see it fur yirsel
Every individual hus tae realize
Her hale fortune isnae in men's eyes,
Say enough is enough
Away and get stuffed.

In the Beginning

There was this man alone
In a beautiful garden.
Stark bollock naked
(Scuse my French, beg your pardon)

He was, yes, the original Nature's Gentleman.
He was in tune, at one, with nature
And the lion lay down with the lamb,
Each peaceable creature
Knew its place in the Order of Things
(And if God meant men to be angels
He'd have given them wings).

The climate was brilliant
The weather was sunny
The whole land flowed with
Milk and honey
Soothing fragrant grasses

Waved verdant in the breeze
Breadfruit baked itself in the sun
And fell out of the trees
Where, by the way, songbirds were singing
With bees for a backing
– Oh a right bed of roses!
But there was Something Lacking . . .

He couldny put his finger on it,
He was in a right tizz.
But, the Lord Our God being a Male God,
He knew exactly whit it wis . . .

A slave.

And soon she was worn to a frazzle
Waiting on His Nibs
Ironing his figleaves
Barbecueing his ribs
While home came the hunter
With the Bacon for the table
She was stuck raising Cain
And breastfeeding Abel.
Him: The Big Breid-winner
Her: A Machine for breedin'
Barescud and pregnant?
Some Garden of Eden!
The sort of sexist division of labour
That went out with the Ark –
i.e. the nuclear family –
Bugger that for a Lark.

So they were both Ripe for Revolting
When that Slimy Serpent came
But – would you Adam and Eve it? –
She got the blame.

Oh Eve took the rap
Eve got framed
Eve was the fall-girl
She got the blame.

The Ballad of Mary Shelley's Creature

The man who made him – not the monster –
Was the man called Frankenstein.
He said I'll try it by Science not Sorcery
Till the Secret of Life is mine.

So Frankenstein to College went
Abandoned Alchemy,
Found himself a famous Professor
Of Natural Philosophy.

Long, long in the Laboratory,
And at the Dissecting Table –
He'll find the Mystery that is Man
If anyone is able.

And deep deep in the dustiest books
From off the highest shelves –
He's made a pledge to wrest knowledge
Where no man safely delves.

And late, late in the Charnel House
Where pale cadavers grin
He's unwound the worms that feed on the flesh
When Death shall let them in.

Among pockmarked victims of the plague
And cut up casualties of War
Dead for weeks, or with the flush still in their cheeks
He's mined for precious ore

He's tinkered with the mechanics of muscles,
Tightened sinews in between.
He might, who knew the machine that was Man,
Make a man of a machine?

But he couldn't cultivate a homunculus
Or jerk him with the galvanist's jolt –
Till the simple secret struck him
Clean as a lightning bolt.

Thus Frankenstein has stolen the spark
That makes all the living draw breath.
He knows that who can once create Life
Soon may triumph over Death.

He clinks his glass against a test tube,
Toasts the Triumph of the Will
And the bloodiest stash of his most ghoulish cache
Is grist to his ghastly mill.

And long, long, in the laboratory
As late as he is able
With a Hellish dolly-rag of a Charnel-House bag
Stretched out on the table.

His brow is of the abattoir,
The jawbone of an ox,
Limb by limb he's constructed him –
Ten foot two in his socks.

He's threading up his backbone beads
Stitches his hide with a pleat and a tuck
From discarded spare parts of the surgeon's Dark Arts
Makes him arms like a fork-lift truck

He has a bolt in his neck and a zip in his cheek
And a ripped off shroud for a quilt –
Nature's assembly line may be all very fine
But this is custom-built,

Correct to every last living detail,
Oiled in every working part.
He has a clockwork brain resistant to pain –
But a resurrected human heart.

Frankenstein smiles down on his creature,
Feels himself to be without blame.
He's going to pull that lever and nothing will ever,
Ever be the same.

Lady of Shalott

Fifteen or younger
she moons in the mirror.
Penny for your thoughts,
Lady of Shalott.
In her bedroom tower
with mother and father
watching T.V. downstairs,
she moons in the mirror
and swears she will never
lead a bloody boring life like theirs.

Maybe you'll find True Romance
at the youth club dance,
Lady of Shalott.

She paints her nails scarlet,
she moons in the mirror.
Ingenue or harlot?
The mirror is misted,
every mirror image twisted.
Like Real Life – but larger.
That kid-glove
dream love
a Knight on a Charger.
Sure
you can lure
him, keep him enslaved.
Buy him Christmas aftershave.

She moons in the mirror
asks it to tell her

she's every bit as pretty as the other
gadfly girls.
Yes, you'll tangle him in your curls,
my Lady of Shalott.

Maybe tonight's the night for
True Romance.
You'll find him at the youth club dance,
Lady of Shalott.

But alas
no handsome prince to dare
ask Rapunzel to let down her hair.
Her confidence cracked from side to side,
by twelve o'clock her tattered pride
is all Cinders stands in.
You're the wallflower the fellows all forgot,
Lady of Shalott.
Oh, how she wishes she could pass
like Alice through the looking glass.
You're waiting to be wanted,
my fairy-tale haunted
Lady of Shalott.

Silver dance shoes in her pocket,
no one's photo in her locket,
home along through the night,
on either side suburban gardens lie,
bungalows and
bedded boxed-in couples high and dry.
But you're
lovely in the lamplight,
my Lady of Shalott.

Advice to Old Lovers

How to be the perfect Old Love. The etiquette?
Well, smile at her a smile that hints at gentle but infinite
regret
(When you bump into her, years later, at, say, one-of-the-old
crowd's 'Big Four O')
Project a certain sense of 'if-you'd-known-then-what-now
you-know . . .'
Suggest (wordlessly) that once upon a time you were a lucky
so-and-so,
Then, when she loved you better than she should of
And you were so mad about her that it was for the good of
Both of you, really, that you split, but – once, oh yes, you
could of . . .

That should go down well. Well, you know women . . .
Do dance with her by all means. To – e.g. – 'Still Crazy
After All These Years' by Paul Simon and she'll be swimming,
I guarantee it, in sentimental, partly alcohol-induced
nostalgia and hazy
But potent memories of how, together, you were terrific.
Please, though, have the manners to refrain from anything
too tastelessly *specific*,
Do steer clear of anything that might embarrass
On your little light-and-laughing sorties down Memory Lane.
Don't remind her of that night on the hearthrug after 'Last
Tango in Paris'
Well, nobody wants to go raking all *that* up again.
No apologies. No post-mortems. As Billie Holliday will have
it: Don't Explain.

No 'I-didn't-mean-to-hurt-yous'. Nothing worse.

If you broke her heart have the grace to imply that, the way
                    you remember it, it was quite the reverse.
Some subtler variation on 'We-were-My-God-*wild*-together
                    but-quite-incompatible,
You-drove-me-mad-it-was-impossible!'
That's the line to take. It flatters both,
Is more morale-boosting all round than the truth.

– And gentle ego-stroking's what it's *for*. (You might just
                    mention
Her Bloke and Your Wife are getting a touch jealous of the
                    attention
You are paying each other, but what the hell –
You always loved each other not wisely but too well . . .)

Don't tell her current Younger Man that she was brilliant at
                    the Twist . . .
Do be married to someone who has an even worse record than
                    her as a Weight Watchers recidivist.
But, please, be Ageing Well yourself, not sad, seedy or pissed,
Or boring, or balding, or wearing a nylon shirt –
To find an Old Love *ludicrous*, that's what would hurt!
Well, nobody likes to think they misspent their Misspent
                    Youth
With someone they can't-see-what-they-once-saw-in-and
                    that's-the-truth.
The last thing she wants is to see her current love laughing up
                    his sleeve –
('*That's* the guy you tried to slit your wrists over? I find that
                    hard to believe!
You were six months on Valium? It almost did you in?
That's the guy who Really Made the Coloured Lights Spin?')

No: if your Brief Re-encounter is to be entirely mutually
                    delightful and not at all stressful
You ought, really, to be almost (but not quite) as handsome
                    and successful
As the Man In Her Life Now, if this can be arranged.
And – if you ever loved her – *tell her she hasn't changed.*

Sexual Etiquette

Sexual etiquette,
Sexual etiquette
How to get more of it
And get more out of what you get.

I wonder if you realize
How across this once proud nation
Night-in night-out
There's thousands of women on the receiving end
Of premature ejaculation.

See there's women knowing what they want
But being too shy to mention
So that what ought to be
A fountain of joy
Is more of a bone of contention.

Sexual etiquette,
Sexual etiquette
How to get more of it
And get more out of what you get.

How to ask – very nicely –
Yet sufficiently precisely.

If your husband tends to kiss you
As if you were his auntie,
If he thinks that a clitoris
Is a flowering potted plant, he

Really *needs* sexual etiquette,
Sexual etiquette
How to (a) get more of it
And (b) get more out of what you get.

If he's rolled over and snoring while you're
Screaming 'Not yet',
If it's a romantic anniversary but he tends to forget,
If he treats you like you're
a refugee from 'Auf Wiedersehen Pet',
He needs sexual etiquette,
Sexual etiquette.

Song for a Dirty Diva

Why are my friends all friends of Dorothy?
Now, I'm cool and glib about gay lib
But suddenly it's got to me
That all of my friends are friends of Dorothy.

Now, I get on great in gay bars and the boys adore me –
We even fancy the same film stars and the crack is frank and
                                                    free.
They'll do my clothes, my hair, my decor
But they won't Do Me.

Yet I can go some from here to Kingdom Come.
Hey, man, you must be barmy
If you think you could exhaust me, yeah, you and
Whose army?
I could ball a rugby team and cream them all to orgasm.
Take a caveman, and his club, to fill ma yawnin chasm.

All those guys who're Really Nice, but not inter-ested,
All those Nancies who don't fancy the tried and tested,
Who turn the other cheek and spurn
What can't be bested,
Oh they huff and they puff and they get real vexed
About my mainstream addiction to
Hetero-sex.

My thoroughly modern girlfriends all say to me
You ain't tried it don't knock it you should suck it and see.
I say thanks a lot but no thanks
It's Not for Me.

I want a real man with a rock hard dose of the horn
Who these days is as rare as
A unicorn.
Oh I wish he'd pure skewer ma penetralia
And spatter ma sheets with a map of Australia

But 'cause all my pals who are gals
Are strictly Sapphic
They seem to deem it disgusting and pornographic.
But my sex life's at a standstill –
There is no through traffic
So – at the risk of sounding politically incorrect –
I need a crash course collision
With something erect.

Yet all of my friends are friends of Dorothy,
Yeah, friends of Dorothy.
Now, I'm cool and glib about gay lib
But suddenly it's got to me
That all of my friends are friends of Dorothy.
And why oh why do they get that vexed
About my mainstream addiction to
Hetero-sex?

My Way

I only did it for a laugh
I did it because I'm a fool for love
I did it because push had come to shove
I did it because – my age – I've got nothing to prove

But I did it
I did it
I did it
Yes I did

I did it to settle an argument with a friend
I did it to drive our Hazel round the bend
I did it to get one over on our kid
I did it to nip it in the bud
I did it that way because I couldn't stand the sight of blood

But I did it
I did it
I did it
Yes I did

I did it to bury the hatchet and get a night's sleep
I did it to get out before I was in too deep
I did it to piss on his chips and put his gas at a peep

But I did it
I did it
I did it
Mea absolutely culpa, me!

I did it to go out in a blaze of glory
I did it to make them listen to my side of the story
I only did it to get attention
I did it to get an honourable mention
I did it to put an end to it all
I did it for no reason at all

But I did it
I did it
I did it
Yes I did

WILLIE RODGER was born 03/03/30 in Kirkintilloch and educated at Lenzie Academy, then Glasgow School of Art from 1948 till 1953. He graduated with a D.A. in Graphic Design and, after a brief unhappy time in London as a commercial artist, took up schoolteaching, becoming Principal Teacher of Art at Clydebank High School from 1968 until his resignation in 1987.

As well as being a painter and a printmaker in lino and woodcut, Willie is a designer of murals and other artefacts such as mugs and beermats. He was comissioned to design a set of Scottish historical playing cards; there's a hundred-foot enamel mural in Glasgow's Exhibition Station, and his stained glass windows for St Mary's Parish Church in Kirkintilloch received Saltire Awards in Art and Architecture 1984–89.

He was the first printmaker to be elected ARSA in 1989, to the RGI in 1994 and he was awarded an honorary doctorate from Stirling University in 1999. His work is in collections all over Britain including the Victoria & Albert Museum, the BBC and P&O Ferries. He exhibits mainly in Edinburgh's Open Eye Gallery.

Willie is married to illustrator Anne Henry, and has two sons, two daughters and ten grandchildren.